Handwriting
Activity Book

for ages 10-11

This CGP book is bursting with fun activities to build up children's skills and confidence.

It's ideal for extra practice to reinforce what they're learning in primary school. Enjoy!

Handwriting Hints

Here are some tips to help you keep your writing neat:

1. Letters of the same type should be the same size:
   - small letters (like c and o) should all be the same height
   - the tops of tall letters (like k and l) should go up to the same height
   - the tails on letters like g and y should be the same length
   - capital letters should be the same height as tall letters

 2. Remember that a 't' is a bit shorter than tall letters.

3. Keep the downstrokes of letters straight and make sure they tilt by the same amount.

4. Try to keep the spaces between words even.

 5. Make sure your writing rests on the line.

6. Don't rush. Take your time and concentrate on keeping your writing as neat and tidy as possible.

> Sometimes you need to use different types of handwriting for different texts.
>
> For example, you might use:
> - non-joined handwriting — for quick notes or a diagram
> - capitals — for headings and subheadings
>
> There are some exercises to practise using different types of handwriting at the end of this book.

Every school has its own handwriting style. Some schools may form letters and joins differently to how they're written here. Check with the school to see how they write and join each letter.

Contents

Conjunctions	2
Homophones	4
Synonyms and antonyms	6
Formal writing	8
Informal writing	10
Writing dialogue	12
Puzzle: Tomb explorers	14
Holiday lists	16
Diary of an astronaut	18
A pet speech	20
The mysterious cave	22
A dreamy poem	24
Giant's Causeway factfile	26
Birthday note-making	28
Answers	30

Published by CGP

Editors: Andy Cashmore, Helen Clements, Alex Fairer, Becca Lakin, Nathan Mair

With thanks to Rachel Craig-McFeely and Alison Griffin for the proofreading.

With thanks to Alice Dent for the copyright research.

ISBN: 978 1 83774 038 3

Printed by Elanders Ltd, Newcastle upon Tyne.
Graphics used on the cover and throughout the book from Corel®
Cover design concept by emc design ltd.

Text, design, layout and original illustrations
© Coordination Group Publications Ltd. (CGP) 2023
All rights reserved.

Photocopying this book is not permitted, even if you have a CLA licence.
Extra copies are available from CGP with next day delivery • 0800 1712 712 • www.cgpbooks.co.uk

Conjunctions

How It Works

Co-ordinating conjunctions join two main clauses together.

and   **yet**   **so**

Subordinating conjunctions join a subordinate clause to a main clause.

after   **though**   **so that**

Now Try These

1. Can you write out these conjunctions?

   _or_   _while_   _before_

   since   _but_   _however_

2. Here are some sentences that use co-ordinating conjunctions.
   Circle the conjunctions then write each sentence on the line below it.

   George likes dragons yet dragons hate George.
   _____

   Najma won the race so she received first prize.
   _____

   I sprinted down the corridor for I was late.
   _____

   Liam plays the piano but he's not very good.
   _____

3. Circle the subordinating conjunctions in these sentences.
   Then write the sentences out as neatly as possible.

   The camel walked until she found water.

   Amjad went out once his delivery had arrived.

   Lily felt very excited when the show began.

   The rocket will leave even if there's no one on it.

   Although penguins are birds, they cannot fly.

An Extra Challenge

Here are some pictures. For each one, write two sentences describing what is happening. Use a different conjunction in each of your sentences.

Make sure you write your sentences in your neatest joined up handwriting.

How confident are you with conjunctions? Tick a box.

Homophones

How It Works

Homophones are words that sound the same, but are spelt differently and have different meanings.

An isle is an island. → *isle*   *aisle* ← An aisle is a narrow walkway between seats.

Now Try These

1. Copy these pairs of homophones onto the lines below.

   soul   *ascent*

   sole   *assent*

2. Can you copy out these sentences that contain pairs of homophones?

   I need to check that I've signed the cheque.

   My heavy throne was thrown by the prince.

   The sealing on the bathroom ceiling has cracked.

   The bus was stationary by the stationery shop.

   At the steel factory, Soph will steal the files.

3. Here are some more sentences that contain pairs of homophones. Can you circle each homophone and then write out the sentences?

Finding the puzzle piece would bring her peace.

I was bored of playing the board game.

The effect of the injury won't affect her speed.

The lost bridal party wandered up the bridle path.

The jeans with the torn waist ended up as waste.

The frustrated vicar had to alter the wonky altar.

An Extra Challenge

Carl has written a report about a brand new type of creature he's discovered, but he's used the wrong homophone in each sentence. Rewrite the sentences with the right homophone using neat, joined up writing.

It has antlers like a mousse but much larger.

The creature has enormous sharp clause that rip through stone.

It has extremely long legs like a flamingo and lives in the dessert.

It is rare to see this animal out and about in the mourning.

Do you feel ~~grate~~ great about these pages? Tick a box.

Synonyms and antonyms

How It Works

Synonyms are words that have the same meaning. Antonyms are words that are opposites.

brave   fearless   afraid

These are synonyms.   These are antonyms.

Now Try These

1. Circle the pair of words that are synonyms. Then copy out each word onto the lines.

    observant   peculiar

    ignorant   eccentric

2. Can you circle the pair of synonyms in each sentence? Then copy out the sentences.

    Selma researched what Brad had investigated.

    The horde of gulls pestered the crowd of people.

    We were satisfied that everyone else was content.

    A really tiny kitten is inside the very large hat.

    They always agitate and irritate each other.

3. Circle the pair of antonyms in each sentence and then copy out the sentences.

As the magician vanished, a dove appeared.

They used to be allies, but now they are enemies.

The centre of town is noisier than the outskirts.

She calmly listened to the man screeching angrily.

The coarse fabric scratched her soft skin.

We often buy pizza, but seldom buy chips.

An Extra Challenge

Match each word in the balloons to its synonym and antonym below, and write them out. Then write two sentences that each include a word from the balloons and either its synonym or antonym. Use your neatest joined up handwriting.

Synonyms

enthusiastic · severe
spotless · substantial
modern · flexible

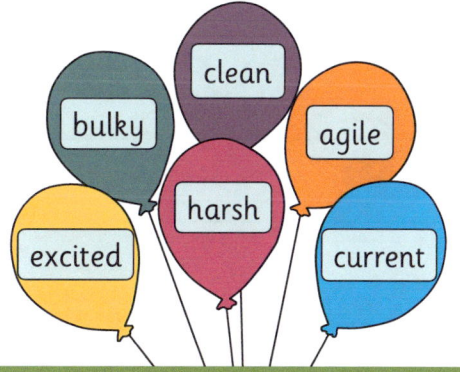

Antonyms

filthy · compact
indifferent · stiff
ancient · lenient

Were these pages enjoyable? Fun? Pleasing? Tick a box.

Formal writing

How It Works

You should use formal writing for serious texts and when you're writing to someone you don't know well. Formal writing should sound polite and impersonal.

Use the subjunctive to talk about things that could or should happen.

Were it raining, I still **would not** feel **sorrow**.

Don't use contractions.   Use formal vocabulary.

Now Try These

1. Can you copy out these formal sentences on the lines below?

   We cannot thank you enough for your honesty.

   Had I been prompt, she would have been calm.

   She will remain in Italy for the foreseeable future.

   He has vowed to avoid consuming lettuce.

   If I were to be rude, they would be aggrieved.

2. Copy out these passages that use formal writing on the lines below.

My presence was requested at a party, but I was uncertain as to whether I should attend. It was possible that it could have been entertaining.

On the other hand, I felt fatigued, so I decided to stay at home. Had I attended the party, I would not have returned home until late at night.

An Extra Challenge

The Polite-Bot 6000 can make informal words and phrases sound more formal, but it struggles with some language. Can you make these phrases formal and write them out?

- If she was earlier...
- If it had been cold...
- you've been
- can't go
- loads of
- Let's...
- well chuffed
- pop in
- It's rubbish that...

Bop! Use your neatest joined up writing. Beep!

Now write three formal sentences. Use at least one of your formal phrases per sentence.

Were those pages marvellous? Put a tick in one of the boxes.

Informal writing

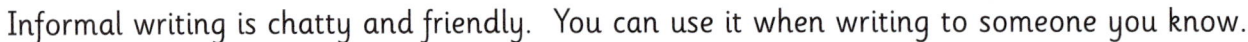

How It Works

Informal writing is chatty and friendly. You can use it when writing to someone you know.

Use informal vocabulary.

She'll be gutted, won't she?

Use contractions. Use questions at the end of a statement.

Now Try These

1. Can you write out these informal sentences?

   Paul had a rubbish swim this morning.

   Maria's jokes are wicked, aren't they?

   This is the yummiest cake I've ever had.

   Jing shouldn't put up with Kristina's bad manners.

   You reckon we're joking, don't you?

   I fancy having a little boogie tonight.

2. Copy this informal passage on the lines below.

   Hey there everyone. I'm so excited to show you this fab new skating trick. I bet you can't wait to see it, can you?

3. Now have a go at copying this longer informal passage.

   Marcus was mad about the footy, wasn't he? His team were well rubbish and he messed up a penalty. They usually play loads better than that!

An Extra Challenge

Gavin has written a letter to his friend, but his older sister thinks it is too formal. Rewrite the sentences below to make them informal. Use neat, joined up handwriting.

- I had the most extraordinary time at the theme park yesterday.
- My father accompanied me on numerous rollercoasters.
- Had I brought more money, I would have purchased candyfloss.
- Upon arriving back at my home, I desired nothing more than to return to the theme park.

You'll tick a box to show how you got on, won't you?

Writing dialogue

How It Works

Dialogue can be written as direct speech. Direct speech is the words that someone says. It goes inside inverted commas and the first word begins with a capital letter.

"I love cheese," he said.

Reported speech shows what someone said without directly quoting the person. It doesn't use inverted commas.

He said that he loves cheese.

Now Try These

1. Copy out the direct speech. Don't forget to include the punctuation.

   "I have violin practice tonight," Ben said.

   "Can you see the otter," asked Fay, "in the river?"

   Kabir replied, "We're going on a cruise in June."

2. Can you copy these lines of reported speech?

   Erin moaned that she hated her new cactus.

   He claimed that his bedroom was very tidy.

3. Tick the box next to the sentence that uses direct speech. Then copy both sentences.

Pedro said he can juggle many balls. ☐

"He definitely cannot," Leila mumbled. ☐

4. Copy out this dialogue between two friends.

"Where is the pizza restaurant?" Ann asked.
"Over there," Kazuo said. "Next to the aquarium."
"Thank goodness, I'm ravenous!" cried Ann.
Kazuo announced that he would try every pizza.

An Extra Challenge

Jessie has written some dialogue for her short story, but some of the punctuation is wrong. Can you rewrite the passage, using the right punctuation and joined up writing?

> "I don't want to go into the haunted mansion"! Chrissie exclaimed.
> It'll be fun. Are you frightened? Joe asked.
> "No, but, Chrissie whispered, people have gone missing in there."
> Joe gasped, then said. "Hang on, something is opening the door…"

Add an extra line of dialogue from Chrissie to reveal what is behind the door.

"Tick a box to show how you did," requested the nice book.

Tomb explorers

A team of archaeologists have uncovered the tomb of an ancient king. They want to find the king's burial chamber, but there are lots of dangers and locked doors in their way. Help them get to the king's chamber by completing the tasks. Use your neatest joined up writing.

1. Circle the conjunction in each sentence. Write out the sentence that makes sense.

   The door opens when knocked five times.

   The door responds to commands, but just say "Open!".

   _____

   _____

2. Circle the right homophone in each box, and then rewrite the whole sentence using the right homophones.

   To avoid making a [dissent / descent] into the spike pit, only step on the [plane / plain] white tiles, or the [floor / flaw] will collapse.

   _____

   _____

   _____

3. Circle the pair of antonyms in this sentence. Then rewrite the sentence, replacing one of the antonyms with a synonym.

   To open this hideous door, you must use the pretty key.

   _____

   _____

4. In each sentence, circle the first and last word that should be contained in inverted commas. Then rewrite the sentences with the correct punctuation.

Watch out for the darts! yelled Jake.

Liv shouted back Activate the lever and enter the tunnel!

_____
_____
_____
_____

5. Circle the informal words in these sentences. Rewrite the sentences using formal language.

Our mates ascended the ramp, which wasn't a brill idea. A large boulder nearly splatted them.

_____
_____
_____

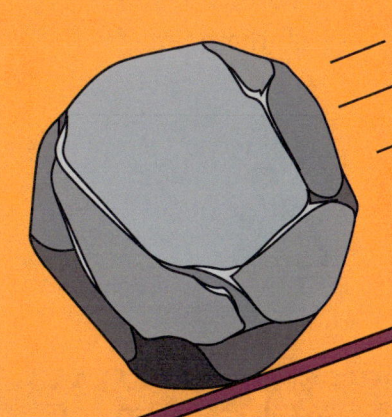

Find five words in the wordsearch that you have circled in the previous tasks. Then add the words to the sentence below to find out how to enter the king's burial chamber.

A	C	O	A	S	I	P	L	A	T	W	P	E	U
F	A	C	T	I	V	A	T	E	S	C	R	N	I
L	L	U	G	L	I	R	T	U	N	N	E	L	D
U	A	O	D	E	S	S	E	T	D	M	T	A	Y
N	D	X	O	S	A	C	N	E	M	A	T	E	S
E	T	R	F	R	S	P	L	A	R	K	Y	W	O

You must _____ the _____ crystals to open a _____ in the _____ for you and your _____.

15

Holiday lists

How It Works

You can write lists using bullet points or numbers. You can punctuate lists in different ways, but make sure you use the same punctuation throughout.

Use either capitals or lower case letters at the start of all the points.

I need to buy:
- A suitcase,
- Sunglasses,
- Toothpaste.

You can use a colon to introduce a list.

You can use commas or semi-colons, with a full stop after the last point. You can also use no punctuation.

Now Try These

1. Copy out this list. Remember to copy the punctuation too.

   When I go on holiday, I need to take:
   - my swimming costume so I can go in the sea;
   - some sun cream so I don't get burnt;
   - a book to read when we drive in the rental car;
   - my camera to take pictures of interesting places.

2. Now copy out this numbered list.

   While on holiday, we are going to:
   1. Go on a boat and find some dolphins
   2. Visit an ancient castle with a drawbridge
   3. Relax by the pool and sunbathe
   4. Play lots of table tennis at the hotel
   5. Walk to the beach and swim in the sea

An Extra Challenge

Two lists about two different holidays have been mixed up. Work out which list items belong in which holiday. Then write the lists out, one as a numbered list and the other using bullet points. Use joined up writing and think about the punctuation you use in both lists.

While I'm in Antarctica, I will:

- visit the museum and art gallery
- use binoculars to watch penguins from afar
- go to the fancy restaurant at the top of the tower

During my city break, I plan to:

- camp in the chilly wilderness
- look round as many shops as possible
- ski down a really steep hill

Do you need a well-earned break after all that? Tick a box.

Diary of an astronaut

How It Works

You can use diaries to write about past events, and your thoughts and feelings. Diary entries are written in the past tense and in the first person.

Try to spot the informal language and reported speech in the diary entry below.

Now Try These

1. Can you copy out this diary entry from an astronaut?

   Dear diary,
   Our journey to planet Yurgox has taken ages and we've avoided many dangers along the way. At one point, we had to dodge a massive meteor. There were loads of great things about the trip too though. My favourite was seeing Earth from space. It was tiny, like a blue marble. Jo said the view was so amazing that she didn't sleep a wink.

2. Copy the next part of the diary entry onto the lines below.

The aliens living on Yurgox have been very kind to us. They've shown us around their capital city, which is powered by nuclear space rocks. We then had a banquet with many peculiar foods. Viktor told me he was given something that looked like grey sludge and tasted of sprouts. I'm pretty glad I didn't try that one!

An Extra Challenge

An astronaut finds an alien's diary carved into a cave wall, but the cave is about to collapse. Copy the diary entry as quickly and neatly as possible, using joined up writing.

Minutes until cave collapses:

Dear diary,

The scientists working in the centre of the planet got in touch with me today to say they had finished their new creation. I travelled there as fast as I could. When I arrived, they all looked very pleased. They unveiled a gigantic rocket that's ready to take us to Earth. I'm incredibly excited to ride in it!

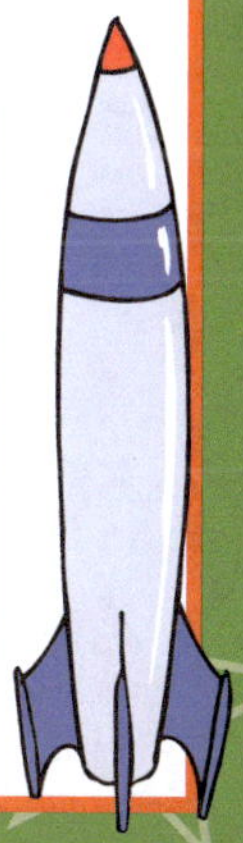

Did you rocket through those pages? Give a box a tick.

A pet speech

How It Works

This formal speech will give you some more practice at copying longer passages.

As you read the speech, think about how it uses formal language.

Now Try These

1. Copy out the first section of this formal speech onto the lines below.

   I am here today to argue that children should be allowed to bring their pets into school. Firstly, studies show that animals can reduce stress, so having pets in school would help pupils feel happy, relaxed and calm. Children who are less stressed are also able to work better. Shouldn't we do everything we can to help children learn?

2. Can you copy the rest of the speech onto the lines below?

> Furthermore, having pets in the classroom would allow children to learn more about different animals. For example, students would learn how to look after pets and observe how they behave. In addition, children will have more fun with pets in the classroom, leading to a more enjoyable learning environment.

An Extra Challenge

Obi is planning a speech about why school uniforms should be banned. Can you use the notes below to write a short speech for him? Use neat, joined up writing.

- uniforms make everyone look the same, which is dull
- they can be expensive
- they are unsuitable for physical activities at break time

Remember to use formal language.

Are you feeling paw-sitive about these pages? Tick a box.

The mysterious cave

How It Works

Try testing your handwriting skills with this detective story.

As you read the story, look out for conjunctions.

Now Try This

1. Copy out this section of a story about a detective onto the next page.

    The robbers swiftly entered the cave and Yas followed at a distance. It was pitch black inside but the robbers used torches to light their way. Although she struggled to see, Yas noticed the robbers disappear through a door in the rock wall. As the door started to close, Yas sprinted desperately towards it. She only just managed to squeeze through before it slammed shut.

    On the other side of the door was a tunnel. After Yas regained her breath, she followed the gleam of the robbers' torches ahead. Suddenly, the glow disappeared. Yas stopped in a panic when she realised she couldn't see a thing.

    Then, a brilliant white light flooded the tunnel and Yas heard heavy footsteps echoing behind her. She turned around slowly...

_____

(blank lined writing space)

An Extra Challenge

Write the next part of the story using the plot points in the boxes below to help you. Use at least one conjunction for each plot point and try to choose a different conjunction each time. Use your neatest joined up handwriting.

| Yas discovers that the person behind her is her best friend. | → | Yas's friend wants Yas to join her gang of robbers. | → | Yas refuses and manages to escape. |

Have you successfully solved these pages? Tick a box.

A dreamy poem

How It Works

Great work so far. Now it's time to show off your skills with this poem. Can you spot all the synonyms?

Now Try This

1. Have a go at copying this poem out onto the next page.

> Each night when I sleep I am able to fly,
> I dream that I soar and glide amongst stars,
> With marvellous, delicate, fragile wings,
> I float above houses, mountains and cars.
> I watch as rabbits bound and leap,
> And majestic owls swoop beside me,
> The world comes alive in the darkness of night,
> They're all so wonderful, the things that I see.
> I follow a grand, magnificent stag,
> To places I've never set eyes on before,
> Then I make my way to the sandy coast,
> To view whales and dolphins, miles from shore.
> I feel so free when I dream I can fly,
>   And cheer with joy as I sail through the air,
>   Delighted and gleeful that I can explore,
>   As everyone else lies in bed unaware.

An Extra Challenge

Each line of this poem contains a homophone that has been used wrongly. Copy out the poem with the right homophones using neat, joined up writing.

Then write four more lines that match the rhyme scheme to finish the poem.

I wrote a draught of a letter,
To complement a fabulous queen,
She through a party that was better,
Than any I had ever scene.

Were those pages a dream come true? Tick one of the boxes.

Giant's Causeway factfile

How It Works

Put your skills to the test with this factfile about the Giant's Causeway. Look at how the text has used non-joined capital letters for the heading and subheadings — try to write these letters as neatly as you can.

Now Try This

1. Read the factfile. Then copy it out onto the next page.

   GIANT'S CAUSEWAY

   LOCATION AND OVERVIEW

   The Giant's Causeway is located in County Antrim in Northern Ireland. It is composed of thousands of basalt columns along the coast and is a hugely popular tourist destination.

   THE LEGEND OF THE CAUSEWAY

   Irish mythology states that the columns are the remains of a causeway made by the Irish giant Finn MacCool. He built the path all the way to Scotland so he could fight a Scottish giant.

   THE GEOLOGICAL EXPLANATION

   Scientists believe that the causeway was created millions of years ago by lava escaping from cracks in the ground. As it cooled, it created the columns we see today.

_____

_____

_____

_____

_____

_____

_____

_____

_____

_____

_____

_____

_____

_____

An Extra Challenge

Write a factfile about a fantasy location that you've made up. Use the prompts to help you and include a heading and subheadings.

Use your neatest joined up writing, but remember to use non-joined capital letters for headings and subheadings.

- What is the place called and where is it?
- Who lives there and what do they look like?
- What is it like to live in the place?
- Are there any other interesting facts about it?

Did you lava those pages? Tick one of the boxes.

Birthday note-making

How It Works

Nice work, you've reached the final pages of handwriting practice.

These party-themed notes will test your non-joined writing skills.

Now Try These

1. Poppy has designed her own birthday cake for her upcoming party. Copy the annotations onto the diagram below using non-joined writing.

cherries and cream garnish

chocolate and caramel sauce

vanilla sponge

sprinkle of toffee pieces

strawberry filling with fresh slices of strawberry

layer of sweet cherry icing

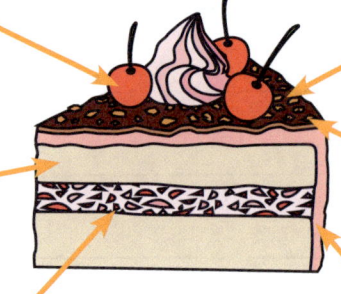

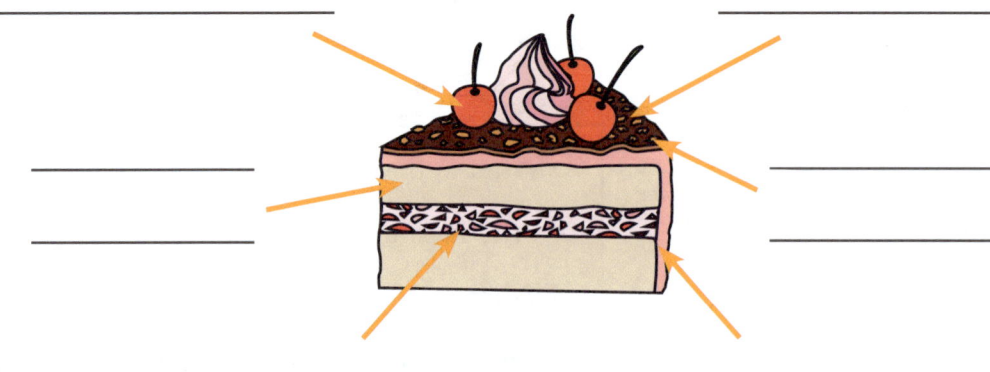

2. Below are Poppy's planning notes for her party.
   Can you copy them out using non-joined writing onto the lines below?

   Date: Saturday 9th September
   Location: 23 Lowood Close, Yewbridge
   Time: 1pm until 4.30pm
   Theme: pirates or carnival
   Guest list: everyone in Year 6
   Activities: board games, karaoke, dancing
   Food: pizza, hot dogs, crisps, salad, cupcakes
   Decorations: balloons, banners, bunting
   Music: the party playlist my sister has made

An Extra Challenge

Can you plan your own party? Start by drawing the birthday cake you'd like to have and annotate it. Then make some notes to plan your day — choose the location, time, theme and other details. Use Poppy's plans in questions one and two to help you.

Remember to use neat, non-joined writing for your notes.

Do you feel like celebrating? Put a tick in one of the boxes.

Answers

Here are the answers to the Extra Challenges and the puzzle.

Pages 2-3 — Conjunctions

Any sensible sentences describing the pictures, with a different conjunction in each one.
E.g. I was fishing <u>even though</u> it was cold outside.
A cow suddenly appeared <u>but</u> she seemed very friendly.

Pages 4-5 — Homophones

It has antlers like a <u>moose</u> but much larger.
The creature has enormous sharp <u>claws</u> that rip through stone.
It has extremely long legs like a flamingo and lives in the <u>desert</u>.
It is rare to see this animal out and about in the <u>morning</u>.

Pages 6-7 — Synonyms and antonyms

excited — enthusiastic, indifferent / bulky — substantial, compact / clean — spotless, filthy / harsh — severe, lenient / agile — flexible, stiff / current — modern, ancient
Any sensible sentences that each include a word from the balloons and either its synonym or antonym.

Pages 8-9 — Formal writing

Any sensible formal version of the phrases, e.g. Had she been earlier… / Had it been cold… / you have been / cannot go / lots of / Let us… / very pleased / enter / It is terrible that…
Any sensible formal sentences that each include at least one of the formal phrases you wrote earlier.

Pages 10-11 — Informal writing

Any sensible informal version of the sentences, e.g. I had the best time ever at the theme park yesterday.

Pages 12-13 — Writing dialogue

"I don't want to go into the haunted mansion!" Chrissie exclaimed.
"It'll be fun. Are you frightened?" Joe asked.
"No, but," Chrissie whispered, "people have gone missing in there."
Joe gasped, then said, "Hang on, something is opening the door…"
Any sensible extra line of dialogue, correctly punctuated.

Pages 14-15 — Tomb explorers

1. You should have circled 'when' and 'but'.
   The door opens when knocked five times.
2. To avoid making a <u>descent</u> into the spike pit, only step on the <u>plain</u> white tiles, or the <u>floor</u> will collapse.
3. You should have circled 'hideous' and 'pretty'.
   Any sensible synonym, e.g. To open this ugly door, you must use the pretty key.
4. You should have circled: Watch, darts, Activate, tunnel.
   "Watch out for the darts!" yelled Jake.
   Liv shouted back, "Activate the lever and enter the tunnel!"
5. You should have circled: mates, wasn't, brill, splatted.
   Any sensible formal version of the sentences.

You must <u>activate</u> the <u>pretty</u> crystals to open a <u>tunnel</u> in the <u>floor</u> for you and your <u>mates</u>.

Pages 16-17 — Holiday lists

You should have written the following lists, with any sensible punctuation, e.g.
While I'm in Antarctica, I will:
1. Camp in the chilly wilderness
2. Use binoculars to watch penguins from afar
3. Ski down a really steep hill

During my city break, I plan to:
- Visit the museum and art gallery;
- Look round as many shops as possible;
- Go to the fancy restaurant at the top of the tower.

Pages 18-19 — Diary of an astronaut

You should have neatly copied the diary entry in joined up writing as quickly as possible.

Pages 20-21 — A pet speech

Any sensible formal speech using the arguments given.

Pages 22-23 — The mysterious cave

Any sensible continuation of the story using the plot points given and at least one conjunction for each plot point.

Pages 24-25 — A dreamy poem

I wrote a <u>draft</u> of a letter,
To <u>compliment</u> a fabulous queen,
She <u>threw</u> a party that was better,
Than any I had ever <u>seen</u>.
Any sensible extra lines that follow the rhyme scheme.

Pages 26-27 — Giant's Causeway factfile

Any sensible factfile using the prompts given.

Pages 28-29 — Birthday note-making

Any sensible diagram of a cake with annotations that are written in non-joined writing. Any sensible party plan with notes that are written in non-joined writing.